# HOMEMADE
# ICE CREAM
# AND SHERBET

# HOMEMADE
# ICE CREAM
# AND SHERBET

## by
## Sheila MacNiven Cameron

**CHARLES E. TUTTLE COMPANY**
**Rutland, Vermont**          **Tokyo, Japan**

REPRESENTATIVES

Continental Europe
BOXERBOOKS, INC.
Zurich

British Isles
PRENTICE-HALL INTERNATIONAL, INC.
London

Australasia
PAUL FLESCH & Co., PTY. LTD.
Melbourne

Canada
M.G. HURTIG LTD.
Edmonton

Published by the Charles E. Tuttle Company, Inc.
of Rutland, Vermont & Tokyo, Japan
with editorial offices at
Suido 1-chome, 2-6, Bunkyo-ku, Tokyo, Japan

Library of Congress catalog card no. 69-16175
International standard book number 0-8048-0258-0

Printed in Japan

to
**LORN**

# CONTENTS

**All the recipes in this collection are designed to make 1¹/₂ quarts, more or less, of ice cream or sherbet.**

# INTRODUCTION

IT'S EVERYONE'S favorite dessert, and the specialty of restaurant chains from coast to coast. Whether one considers it a luxury or a necessity, a delicacy or a staple, almost everyone loves ice cream, and everyone has a favorite flavor.

"Make mine vanilla" has become an American idiom. Chocolate is the second favorite throughout the United States, except in New England, where it is edged out by coffee. (Perhaps this represents a subtle gesture of defiance carried down from Boston Tea Party days!) Philadelphia and Seattle are identified by their vanilla ice creams. Howard Johnson became King-of-the-Road because children could identify the familiar orange-roofed stands and gleefully shout "Twenty-eight flavors!" hoping tired fathers would stop for a few minutes for a creamy cone.

And who has not stood, paralyzed by indecision, trying to make up his mind which delectable flavor to choose from the dazzling array of thirty-three, thirty-eight, or forty flavors listed at one of a chain of roadside ice cream shops? Will it be cantaloupe, rocky road, or peppermint candy? Perhaps a scoop of apricot nut and one of chocolate mint?

Nowadays, children, teen-agers, and adults have rediscovered the entertainment value of making their

**9**

## INTRODUCTION

own ice cream. Not the refrigerator ice cube tray way, but the old-fashioned method, cranked in a tub of crushed ice and rock salt. The resulting ice cream is undeniably superior to the refrigerator kind. It's smoother, lighter, and tastier. And often, it is less fattening. Refrigerator ice creams must rely on a large proportion of whipping cream, egg yolks, or condensed milk to keep them smooth. The crank solves this problem in the "old-fashioned" machine. The freezing process is much faster in the cranked machine than in the ice cube tray, too—minutes as opposed to hours.

One may, of course, use a freezer that has an electric motor to do the work. But how much more fun to let everyone pitch in to take a turn at the hand crank. When the men and boys have demonstrated their muscular prowess for a few minutes each, behold: The ice cream is ready! Faster than a trip to the nearest supermarket. And what a treat! Without the chemicals and stabilizers necessary in commercial products, homemade ice cream tends to melt faster and to taste, somehow, more heavenly.

Is there any better way to have a party? Of course! Use two or three freezers, and make different flavors of ice cream!

# BASIC INSTRUCTIONS
## Equipment

ONCE YOU HAVE your basic equipment, you'll find that ice cream making is not really mysterious or difficult.

First, you'll need an *ice cream freezer,* the kind often referred to in newspapers and catalogs as "an old-fashioned freezer." Whether you select one powered by an electric motor or one that must be cranked by hand is up to you. You can usually find both types in hardware stores, department stores, discount houses, mail order catalogs, large drug stores, stamp redemption centers, and second-hand stores.

If you anticipate being short of man and muscle power at cranking time, by all means buy the electric model. On the other hand, if you live in an area where electric power is uncertain, you'll certainly want the manual model. If you're in doubt, buy the hand crank freezer. It's somewhat less expensive than the electric model, and has fewer problems likely to upset it. Ordinarily, you can expect assistance in the cranking from children or guests.

A *large scoop* or measuring cup will be needed for the ice and salt. A plastic two-cup measure is ideal, but an empty one-pound coffee can will do. You can devise a handy scoop yourself by slicing the bottom off an empty one-quart plastic bleach jug.

## BASIC INSTRUCTIONS

A pile of *old newspapers* or old quilts and blankets are good to have for covering up the freezer, especially if you plan to store your finished ice cream there for several hours.

A *rubber spatula* and a sturdy *ice cream scoop* are handy for getting the ice cream off the dasher and into awaiting dishes. Tablespoons sometimes get weak in the knees and collapse when asked to dig out hard frozen ice cream!

# Procedure

FOR THE ACTUAL FREEZING, you'll need *rock salt* and *crushed ice.* The easiest system is to buy your ice already crushed, at an ice machine or from an ice man, if you can. The next best system is to get a block of ice, an ice pick, and a guest or family member willing to chip the ice into a bucket for you. If you have an ice cube maker and a lot of ice cubes squirreled away in your deep freeze, you may want to use the cubes. However, they will have to be cut down to size if they are to be cooperative. For this job, you use a canvas bag, or old bath towels, rubber mallets, (old croquet mallets will do!) and some young boys who need to work off excess energy pounding the ice. The idea is to get the ice down to pea-sized fragments. If you can find snow outside, you're in luck. Use that.

Place the canister in the freezer tub. Insert the dasher. Pour in the ice cream mixture, filling the canister no more than 3/4 full. Replace canister lid, and attach the crank. Turn it a few times to make sure everything is hooked up properly.

Now, pack the tub 1/3 full of crushed ice. Then begin putting in alternate layers of salt and ice. Your aim is to have 3 to 6 measures of ice for each measure of rock salt. (The larger proportion of salt will freeze the mixture faster, but the smaller proportion of salt will make a finer grained ice cream.)

Let it stand for about five minutes. Then begin cranking slowly. When you begin to feel a slight pull, indicating that the mixture has frozen to the mushy stage (5 to 10 minutes), begin cranking rapidly. If you are to add fruit or other ingredients to the mixture, it is at this point you do it. Continue cranking until the ice cream feels very stiff. The whole process may not take much more than 15 or 20 minutes.

Remove the dasher, using a rubber spatula to scrape off the excess ice cream. The youngest child, or the person who did the most cranking, has the traditional privilege of getting the dasher for "first licks." Memory holds nothing that tastes quite so ambrosial!

# Storage

IF YOU DO NOT PLAN to use all the ice cream immediately, you may cover it with waxed paper, and replace the canister lid. Fit a cork or a tight wad of waxed paper into the hole in the canister lid. Place the canister back in the tub. Drain off excess water, and repack the tub with more ice and salt. Cover the

## BASIC INSTRUCTIONS

whole thing with a thick layer of old blankets or news-papers.

If you prefer, turn the ice cream into molds or plastic containers, cover tightly, and place in your freezer compartment or deep freeze.

# Helpful Hints

ALL THE RECIPES in this collection are designed to make $1^1/_2$ quarts, more or less, of ice cream or sherbet.

A tiny touch of SALT added to any ice cream recipe will help it freeze better.

ALCOHOLIC DRINKS should be used sparingly for flavoring, as they tend to act as anti-freeze.

Making a SYRUP by boiling the water and sugar together first is not necessary, but makes a smoother sherbet.

CORN SYRUP can be used to replace 1/3 of the sugar in most ice cream and sherbet recipes, to obtain smoother results.

CUSTARD BASE ice creams, thickened with flour or egg yolks, usually taste smoother and richer.

Dissolved GELATIN is used to make ice creams and sherbets smoother and lighter.

Instant nonfat DRIED MILK can be added to almost any ice cream recipe to make it smoother, richer tasting, and more nutritious.

Whipped instant nonfat dried milk or evaporated milk can be used in place of heavy cream to make low calorie "ice cream."

# RECIPES
# Ice Creams

### PHILADELPHIA ICE CREAM

This is just about the simplest of all ice cream recipes, and the favorite of many. It's a good recipe for the novice to start with.

> 1 quart half-and-half (half milk, half cream)
> 2 tablespoons vanilla
> 3/4 cup sugar
> 1/8 teaspoon salt
> 1/2 cup instant nonfat dried milk

Mix all ingredients together. Cool. Freeze according to Basic Instructions.

For a richer ice cream, substitute one cup of heavy cream for one cup of the half-and-half.

Some cooks prefer to scald the half-and-half before adding the other ingredients. Chill before freezing.

## ICE CREAM RECIPES

### RENNET ICE CREAM

3 rennett tablets
2 tablespoons cold water
$1^1/_4$ cups sugar
1 quart whole milk
$1^1/_4$ cups heavy cream
$1^1/_2$ tablespoons vanilla

Dissolve the rennet tablets in cold water. Combine the remaining ingredients, and heat to lukewarm (110 degrees), not hot. Stir in the dissolved tablets, and pour into freezer canister. Let stand undisturbed for about five minutes. Chill. Freeze according to Basic Instructions.

This basic recipe can also be used for making various fruit ice creams, too. Omit the vanilla in the basic recipe. When the ice cream is about 3/4 frozen, add 1 cup of mashed, sweetened strawberries, raspberries, or apricots, and 1/4 teaspoon almond extract. Finish freezing.

### VANILLA CUSTARD

2 cups milk
1 tablespoon cornstarch
3/4 cup sugar
1/2 cup dried powdered nonfat milk
2 egg yolks, slightly beaten
1/4 teaspoon salt
1 tablespoon vanilla
2 cups heavy cream

ICE CREAM RECIPES

Scald 1¹/₂ cups of the milk. Mix the cornstarch, sugar, and nonfat milk together, and stir in the remaining ¹/₂ cup of cold milk. Slowly add the scalded milk, and cook, stirring, this mixture over hot water for about 8 minutes. Mix in the egg yolks, and cook 2 or 3 minutes longer. Remove from stove, and cool quickly. Add the salt, vanilla, and heavy cream, and freeze according to Basic Instructions.

Most persons who like frozen custard like it somewhat soft, so don't serve this frozen hard as a brick! "Soft Ice Cream" is a Seattle favorite. For your New England friends, add a tablespoon of instant coffee to the scalded milk.

## BUTTER PECAN ICE CREAM

Prepare your favorite recipe for vanilla ice cream. Begin freezing according to Basic Instructions. When mixture begins to get stiff, add 1 cup of coarsely chopped pecans that have been lightly browned in 3 tablespoons of butter in a heavy pan over low heat. Cool before adding to ice cream! Finish freezing.

## COFFEE ICE CREAM

Dissolve 1 tablespoon of instant coffee in ¹/₄ cup of hot water, and add it to your favorite vanilla ice cream recipe just before freezing. Or add the instant coffee directly to the scalded milk in the frozen custard recipe.

## ICE CREAM RECIPES

If instant coffee isn't available, don't fret! Substitute 1 cup of very strong cold coffee and 1/2 cup dry non-fat milk for 1 cup of milk in almost any basic vanilla ice cream recipe, and continue according to instructions.

### MOCHA CHIP ICE CREAM

Follow instructions for Coffee Ice Cream (page 17), To the chilled mixture, add 1 cup (1 small package of semi-sweet chocolate bits that have been chopped fine. You can chop them on your chopping board, or run them very briefly in your electric blender, but chill the chocolate bits first. Delicious! If you want to get the reputation of being a gourmet, add 1/4 cup fine brandy just before removing the dasher. This could even win you the man of your dreams!

### CHOCOLATE ICE CREAM

2 cups milk
2 squares unsweetened chocolate
1 1/4 cups sugar
1 tablespoon cornstarch
1/4 teaspoon salt
2 eggs, slightly beaten
2 cups heavy cream
1 tablespoon vanilla

Scald 1 1/2 cups of the milk with the chocolate. Mix sugar, cornstarch, and salt together, stir into the remaining 1/2 cup of cold milk, and blend into the scalded milk. Add the eggs, and cook over hot water until slightly thickened. Cool. Add cream and vanilla. Freeze according to Basic Instructions.

### CHOCOLATE CHIP ICE CREAM

Follow instructions for your favorite vanilla ice cream. To the chilled mixture, just before freezing, add 1 cup (1 small package) of semi-sweet chocolate bits that have been chopped fine. You can chop them on your chopping board, or run them very very briefly in your electric blender, but chill them before you do this.

### CHOCOLATE NUT ICE CREAM

To the preceding recipe for Chocolate Ice Cream (page, 18) add 1/2 teaspoon almond extract along with the vanilla. Add one cup of chopped toasted almonds, or other chopped nuts, and freeze according to Basic Instructions.

### CHOCOMINT ICE CREAM

Follow the recipe for Chocolate Ice Cream (page 18), omitting the vanilla, and adding 1/2 teaspoon mint flavoring. Freeze according to Basic Instructions.

### PEPPERMINT STICK ICE CREAM

To any of the basic recipes for vanilla or chocolate ice cream, add 1 cup of crushed peppermint stick candy when the ice cream is about two-thirds frozen.

## ICE CREAM RECIPES

### ROCKY ROAD ICE CREAM

2 cups milk
2 squares unsweetened chocolate
3/4 cup sugar
1/8 teaspoon salt
2 tablespoons vanilla
1/2 cup instant nonfat dry milk
1 cup cream (heavy)
1 cup coarsely chopped nuts
2 cups miniature marshmallows (or cut-up
    large marshmallows)

Scald the milk and the chocolate. Stir in the sugar, salt, vanilla, and nonfat dry milk. Cool. Add the cream, nuts, and marshmallows. Freeze according to Basic Instructions.

This is a particular favorite of small boys—and big boys, too.

### TOASTED COCONUT ICE CREAM

1 can (15 oz.) sweetened condensed milk
1 cup water
2 teaspoons vanilla extract
1/2 teaspoon coconut flavoring, if available
2 cups heavy cream
2 cups shredded coconut

Mix together condensed milk, water, vanilla, coconut flavoring, and cream. Freeze according to Basic Instructions. Spread coconut in shallow pan, and bake in 350 degree F oven for about 15 minutes, stirring

**20**

occasionally. Cool. When ice cream is almost frozen, mix in toasted coconut, and continue freezing.

### FRESH PEACH ICE CREAM

2 cups ripe mashed peaches
2 tablespoons lemon juice
1 cup sugar
1 quart milk
2 cups heavy cream
1/2 cup instant nonfat dried milk
1/8 teaspoon salt
1 teaspoon vanilla
1/4 teaspoon almond extract

Peel, slice, and mash the ripe peaches. Mix in the lemon juice and half the sugar, and set aside. Mix the milk, cream, dried milk, salt, vanilla, almond extract, and the remaining sugar, and freeze according to Basic Instructions. When mixture is slightly firm, add the fruit, and finish freezing. If fruit is tart, you may want to add more sugar, according to your taste.

### FRESH APRICOT ICE CREAM

Follow the directions for Fresh Peach Ice Cream (page 21), substituting puréed or mashed fresh apricots for the peaches.

## ICE CREAM RECIPES

### FRESH QUINCE ICE CREAM

Follow the directions for Fresh Peach Ice Cream (page 21), substituting puréed or mashed fresh quinces for the peaches.

### APRICOT HONEY ICE CREAM

Follow the directions for Fresh Peach Ice Cream (page 21), substituting puréed or mashed fresh apricots for the peaches, and $^1/_2$ cup honey for $^1/_2$ cup of the sugar.

### DRIED APRICOT ICE CREAM

2 cups dried apricots
$2^1/_2$ cups water
$1^1/_2$ cups sugar
2 cups milk
2 cups heavy cream
1/4 teaspoon salt
1/4 teaspoon almond extract
1 teaspoon vanilla

Simmer the apricots and water together until the apricots are very tender. This may take anywhere from ten to thirty minutes, depending on the kind of apricots you have. When they are soft, drain the juice off and measure out one cup of it. Force the apricots through a ricer or a food mill, with the cup of juice, or run them in an electric blender. Add sugar and chill.

Mix apricot purée, milk, cream, salt, almond extract, and vanilla, and freeze according to Basic Instructions.

## APRICOT NUT ICE CREAM

To the preceding recipe, add 1 cup chopped toasted almonds when the ice cream seems to be about two-thirds frozen.

## PEACH BUTTERMILK ICE CREAM

1 tablespoon unflavored gelatin
1/4 cup cold water
2 egg yolks
1 cup sugar
2 cups buttermilk
1/4 teaspoon salt
1 teaspoon vanilla extract
1/4 teaspoon almond extract
2 cups whipping cream
2 cups finely diced freestone peaches

Sprinkle the gelatin on the cold water to soften. Beat egg yolks. Beat in sugar. Heat buttermilk, and gradually pour over the egg yolks, stirring constantly. Stir in the softened gelatin, and cook mixture, stirring constantly, over hot water for about five minutes. Cool. Mix in salt, vanilla, almond extract, and whipping cream, and freeze according to Basic Instructions. When mixture is almost frozen, mix in peaches, and finish freezing.

## ICE CREAM RECIPES

### AVOCADO ICE CREAM

2 medium size, ripe avocadoes
1 teaspoon lemon or lime juice
4 eggs
1 cup sugar
2 cups milk, scalded
2 cups whipping cream

Mash the avocado pulp with a fork. Make sure you scrape all the pulp from the avocado skin, in order to get the nice green color! Blend in the lemon juice. Beat the eggs until thick. Beat in the sugar. Slowly add the scalded milk, and mix well. Cook mixture over hot water, stirring constantly. When custard begins to coat spoon, remove from heat, and chill.

Mix custard, puréed avocado pulp, and whipping cream together, and freeze according to Basic Instructions.

### BUTTERSCOTCH FRAPPE

1 package butterscotch pudding mix
6 cups whole milk
1 cup instant nonfat dry milk
1 cup brown sugar

Don't use the "instant" type of pudding mix! Mix 3 cups of the milk with the pudding mix, and bring to a boil, stirring constantly. Remove from fire. Blend in the nonfat dry milk, brown sugar, and the remaining three cups of milk. Chill well, and freeze according to Basic Instructions.

## BUTTERSCOTCH ICE CREAM

In the preceding recipe, substitute the last 3 cups of milk with 1 cup of milk and 2 cups of heavy cream.

## BANANA ICE CREAM

Use one of the recipes for vanilla ice cream, and when the mixture is partially frozen, mix in 1 cup of well-mashed ripe banana, and 1/4 cup lemon juice. Continue freezing according to Basic Instructions.

## CANTALOUPE ICE CREAM

1 large ripe cantaloupe
1 can sweetened condensed milk (15 oz.)
1/4 teaspoon salt
1 teaspoon vanilla
1/4 teaspoon almond extract
1/2 cup milk
1/4 cup lemon juice
2 cups whipping cream

Cut cantaloupe in half and remove seeds and rind. Mash well and purée in food mill or electric blender. Mix in all remaining ingredients, and freeze according to Basic Instructions.

## ICE CREAM RECIPES

### GEORGE WASHINGTON CHERRY ICE CREAM

Prepare vanilla or vanilla custard ice cream. When mixture is about three-quarters frozen, add one cup of chopped, drained maraschino cherries. Finish freezing.

If you wish, you can serve a teaspoon or two of the maraschino cherry juice over each portion of ice cream, as a "sauce." Just remember that a little bit goes a long way!

### GREEN GAGE ICE CREAM

10 ripe green gage plums
1 cup sugar
1/2 cup water
2 eggs
1 cup scalded milk
2 tablespoons lemon juice
2 cups heavy cream

Cut plums in half and remove seeds. Simmer plums with $1/_2$ cup of the sugar, and $1/_2$ cup water, for about ten minutes, or until quite soft. Purée in electric blender or food mill, or by forcing through sieve. Beat eggs and remaining sugar together until thick. Add scalded milk slowly, stirring constantly. Cool.

Combine plum puree, egg mixture, lemon juice, and heavy cream. Freeze according to Basic Instructions.

### CANDIED GINGER ICE CREAM

2 cups milk
1 teaspoon vanilla
3/4 cup sugar
1/8 teaspoon salt
1/2 cup instant nonfat dried milk
2 cups whipping cream
1/3 cup finely chopped candied ginger

Mix milk, vanilla, sugar, salt, nonfat milk, and whipping cream together, and freeze according to Basic Instructions. When mixture is almost frozen, add the finely chopped ginger, mix in well, and continue freezing.

If you prefer a custard base ice cream, follow a recipe for a basic vanilla one, and add the chopped ginger, as above.

### GUAVA ICE CREAM

4 eggs
1 cup sugar
2 cups milk, scalded
1/3 cup stewed, puréed guavas
2 cups whipping cream

Beat the eggs until thick. Beat in the sugar. Slowly add the scalded milk, and mix well. Cook mixture over hot water until it begins to coat the spoon. Remove mixture from heat, and chill.

Mix the guava purée, the custard mixture, and the whipping cream together. Freeze according to Basic Instructions.

**27**

## ICE CREAM RECIPES

### GRAPE ICE CREAM

1 6-oz. can grape juice concentrate
1/4 cup lemon juice
1 cup sugar
1 quart milk
1 cup heavy cream, whipped

Blend grape juice concentrate, lemon juice, and sugar. Mix with milk. Fold in whipped cream. Freeze according to Basic Instructions.

### LYCHEE ICE CREAM

2 cup ripe, mashed lychees
2 tablespoons lemon juice
1 cup sugar
2 cups milk
1 cup heavy cream, whipped

Mix the fruit, lemon juice, and sugar together well. Add the milk. Fold in the whipped cream. Freeze according to Basic Instructions.

### MANGO ICE CREAM

1 cup ripe mango pulp, puréed
2 tablespoons lemon or lime juice
1 cup sugar
4 eggs
2 cups milk, scalded
2 cups whipping cream

Mix ripe mango purée, lemon juice, and 1/4 cup of the sugar, and set aside. Beat the eggs thick. Beat in the remaining 3/4 cup sugar. Slowly add the scalded milk. Cook mixture over hot water until custard begins to coat spoon. Remove from heat and chill.

Mix custard, mango purée, and whipping cream together, and freeze according to Basic Instructions.

## PUMPKIN CUSTARD ICE CREAM

4 eggs, slightly beaten
1 cup brown sugar, firmly packed
2 cups scalded milk
1 cup canned pumpkin
3 teaspoons pumpkin pie spice
2 cups heavy cream

Beat eggs slightly. Add brown sugar to scalded milk, and stir until dissolved. Gradually pour the scalded milk on the eggs, and continue beating. Mix in the pumpkin, and the spice. Chill mixture. Add the cream, and freeze according to Basic Instructions.

## OLD-FASHIONED STRAWBERRY ICE CREAM

When strawberries are in season, and when money and calories are no object, this is the way to do it!

## ICE CREAM RECIPES

4 cups cleaned sliced strawberries
2 cups sugar
1/8 teaspoon almond extract
2 cups light cream
2 cups heavy cream, whipped

Mash or sieve berries, and mix with sugar and almond extract. Mix in light cream. Fold in whipped cream. Freeze according to Basic Instructions.


## LEMON ICE CREAM

1/3 cup lemon juice
2 teaspoons grated lemon rind
2 cups sugar
2 cups milk
3 tablespoons flour
1/2 cup water
1 cup heavy cream, whipped

Mix lemon juice and lemon rind and set aside. Heat sugar and milk together, stirring to dissolve sugar. Blend flour into cold water until smooth. Add to milk mixture. Cook over low heat until mixture begins to thicken, stirring constantly. Remove from heat. Add lemon juice and rind. Chill. Fold in whipped cream. Freeze according to Basic Instructions.


## LIME ICE CREAM

Follow directions for Lemon Ice Cream (preceding recipe), substituting lime juice and grated lime rind.

## KUMQUAT ICE CREAM

10 preserved kumquats
1/4 cup Curaçao
4 eggs
3/4 cup sugar
2 cups milk, scalded
2 cups whipping cream

Chop kumquats finely, add Curaçao, and set aside. Beat eggs thick, then beat in sugar. Slowly add the scalded milk, and cook mixture over hot water, stirring constantly. When custard begins to coat spoon, remove from heat, and chill.

Mix custard and whipping cream together, and freeze according to Basic Instructions. When mixture is almost frozen, add the chopped kumquats and Curacao, mix in well, and continue freezing until done.

## ORANGE DELICIOUS

2 cups sugar
1 cup water
2 cups orange juice
2 egg yolks
1 cup rich milk or half-and-half
1 teaspoon grated orange rind
1 cup heavy cream, whipped

Boil sugar and water together five minutes. Add orange juice. Beat egg yolks and milk together, and mix in, along with grated orange rind. Chill mixture. Fold in whipped cream, and freeze according to Basic Instructions.

## ICE CREAM RECIPES

### ORANGE AMBROSIA

Prepare recipe for Orange Delicious (preceding recipe). Fold in 1 cup of shredded coconut along with the whipped cream, and freeze according to Basic Instructions. Serve topped with slices of peeled oranges.

### FROZEN HEAVEN

3 cups tiny marshmallows
3 cups orange juice
2 fresh limes
2 cups heavy cream

Heat the marshmallows in the orange juice, stirring constantly, until the marshmallows have all melted. Remove from heat immediately. If no tiny marshmallows are available, cut up large ones with scissors. Add the juice and grated skin from the limes. Chill mixture. It will become thick. Mix in the cream, and freeze according to Basic Instructions.

### BISCUIT TORTONI

6 egg yolks
1/2 cup sugar
$1^1/_2$ cups milk, scalded
1 cup finely crushed macaroons
1/2 cup finely chopped toasted almonds
1 teaspoon vanilla extract
2 cups heavy cream
2 tablespoons sherry

Beat egg yolks until thick and light. Beat in sugar. Gradually add the scalded milk, mixing constantly. Cook this mixture over hot water for five minutes, stirring constantly. Chill.

Mix the cooled custard with the remaining ingredients, and freeze according to Basic Instructions.

This delicious concoction is best served slightly soft, in small paper cups.

## MRS. KINNE'S FROZEN PLUM PUDDING

This old recipe, dating from 1890, is basically a parfait type, and can be frozen in the cranked freezer, or can be packed in molds and frozen "as is."

> 1/2 cup sugar
> 1/2 cup water
> 2 egg whites
> 1/4 cup plumped currants
> 1/4 cup plumbed raisins
> 1/4 cup chopped walnuts or pecans
> 1/4 cup chopped almonds
> 1/2 cup chopped candied cherries
> 1 cup heavy cream, whipped
> 1 teaspoon vanilla

Cook the sugar and water together to the thread stage. Beat egg whites stiff. Pour sugar syrup in fine, steady stream into egg whites, and continue beating constantly. Beat until mixture is quite thick and cool. Fold in the fruits and nuts. Fold in the cream and vanilla. Freeze according to Basic Instructions, or turn into molds and freeze in deep freezer or packed in ice and salt.

# ICE CREAM RECIPES

## NUT PUDDING

This is a very old recipe that comes from the South.
It's expensive, and rich, so save it for special occa-
sions.

> 3/4 cup almonds
> 3/4 cup filberts
> 3/4 cup walnuts or pecans
> 2 cups sugar
> 4 cups rich milk, scalded
> 1 tablespoon vanilla extract
> 1 teaspoon almond extract
> 2 cups whipping cream

Grind the nuts without blanching them. Better yet,
use a blender, if you have one. Mix in the sugar. Add
the scalded milk, and stir till sugar is dissolved. Chill.
Add extracts and whipping cream, and freeze according to Basic Instructions.

## MISSISSIPPI FIG PUDDING

> 1 tablespoon unflavored gelatin
> 1/4 cup cold water
> 3 eggs
> 1 cup sugar
> 2 cups milk, scalded
> 1/8 teaspoon salt
> 1 cup chopped pecans (or walnuts)
> 1/2 cup finely chopped figs
> 2 teaspoons vanilla
> 2 cups whipping cream

Sprinkle the gelatin on the cold water. Beat eggs until thick. Beat in sugar. Pour scalded milk over egg mixture gradually. Cook over hot water for about five minutes, or until mixture coats spoon, stirring constantly. Add the softened gelatin, and stir until melted. Cool. Add salt, nuts, figs, vanilla, and whipping cream. Freeze according to Basic Instructions.

# Sherbets

### LEMON SHERBET

4 cups water
1 1/2 to 2 cups sugar
1 cup fresh lemon juice
1 teaspoon grated lemon rind
3 egg whites
1/8 teaspoon salt

Combine sugar and water, and boil for five minutes. Chill. Use the smaller amount of sugar if your lemons are a sweet variety, such as Meyer. Combine chilled syrup, lemon juice, and lemon rind, and freeze to a mush, according to Basic Instructions. Beat the egg whites and salt stiff. Add, and finish freezing.

## SHERBET RECIPES

### CALAMONDIN SHERBET

Substitute calamondin juice for lemon juice in almost any recipe for lemon sherbet.

### LEMONADE SHERBET

Here's one of the easiest recipes possible, made from ingredients you likely have on hand already. The flavor is deliciously lemony. Mix together, and freeze according to Basic Instructions.

2 $14^1/_2$-oz. cans of evaporated milk
2 cans of frozen lemonade concentrate

### ORANGE SHERBET

2 cups, sugar
2 cups water
2 teaspoons grated orange rind
2 cups orange juice
1/4 cup lemon juice
2 egg whites
1/4 teaspoon salt

Bring sugar and water to a boil, and simmer for two or three minutes. Add orange rind, stir, and set aside to chill. When cooled, add orange juice and lemon juice. Beat egg whites and salt stiff, and fold in. Freeze according to Basic Instructions.

### GRAPEFRUIT SHERBET

2 teaspoons unflavored gelatin
1/2 cup cold water
2 cups sugar
2 cups water
1/2 cup lemon juice
4 cups grapefruit juice
1/2 cup orange juice
2 egg whites, beaten stiff
1/4 teaspoon salt

Soften gelatin in cold water. Bring sugar and water to a boil, and boil until sugar is all dissolved. Melt gelatin in the hot syrup. Chill.

Mix into the chilled syrup the lemon juice, grapefruit juice, and orange juice. Beat egg whites with salt, and fold in. Freeze according to Basic Instructions.

### TROPICAL SHERBET

2 cups sugar
2 cups water
3 ripe bananas, mashed
1 cup orange juice
1/2 cup lime or lemon juice
1 cup pineapple juice or apricot nectar
2 egg whites, stiffly beaten

Boil sugar and water together until sugar is dissolved. Chill. Mix in mashed bananas, orange juice, lime juice, and, very gently, the beaten egg whites. Freeze according to Basic Instructions.

## SHERBET RECIPES

### AVOCADO SHERBET

$1^1/_2$ cups puréed ripe avocado
4 cups buttermilk
1 cup sugar
1 cup light corn syrup
1/3 cup lemon juice

Make sure you scrape all the pulp from the avocado skin, in order to get the nice green color. Mix all ingredients together, and freeze at once according to Basic Instructions.

### RASPBERRY SHERBET

2 cups water
1 cup sugar
2 cups raspberry juice*
1 tablespoon lemon juice
2 egg whites (optional)

Combine water and sugar, and bring to a boil. Boil for five minutes. Chill. Add raspberry juice and lemon juice. Freeze according to Basic Instructions. If desired, fold in two egg whites and 1/8 teaspoon salt, beaten stiff, when mixture is about half frozen, and then finish freezing.

* Use canned or fresh juice. To prepare fresh juice, sprinkle berries lightly with sugar and let stand for two hours. Mash, and strain through cheesecloth. Or, run berries through food mill or electric blender, and sieve out seeds through a fine sieve or cheesecloth.

# SHERBET RECIPES

### BLACKBERRY SHERBET
### BLUEBERRY SHERBET
### BOYSENBERRY SHERBET
### LOGANBERRY SHERBET
### STRAWBERRY SHERBET

Follow directions for Raspberry Sherbet (preceding recipe). Adjust amount of sugar to sweetness or tartness of berries.

### CANTALOUPE SHERBET

4 ripe cantaloupes
1/2 teaspoon salt
1 cup sugar
1/3 cup lemon juice
Dash or two of angostura bitters
2 egg whites, stiffly beaten

Halve melons, remove seeds, and scoop out ripe pulp. Press pulp through a sieve or food mill, or run in an electric blender. Mix in salt, sugar, lemon juice, and bitters. Chill well. Add egg whites, and freeze according to Basic Instructions.

### CIDER SHERBET

2 cups sweet apple cider
1 cup sugar
1 tablespoon lemon juice
1/8 teaspoon salt
2 egg whites.

## SHERBET RECIPES

Mix cider, sugar, and lemon juice, and freeze according to Basic Instructions. When mixture is partially frozen, add the egg whites and salt, which have been beaten stiff. Finish freezing.

### CRANBERRY SHERBET

4 cups fresh cranberries
2 cups water
3 cups sugar
1 cup orange juice
1 tablespoon grated orange rind
2 egg whites
1/8 teaspoon salt

Clean cranberries, cover with sugar and water, bring to a boil, and boil for about four minutes, stirring constantly. Cool. Put cranberries through a food mill or electric blender. Add the orange juice and rind. Freeze according to Basic Instructions until mixture is about half frozen, or mushy. Beat egg whites and salt stiff, and fold in. Finish freezing.

### SURINAM CHERRY SHERBET

You may know these red, ribbed cherries as "Florida cherries" or "Pitangas."

2 cups Surinam cherry juice*
4 cups water
2 cups sugar
1/2 cup lime juice
1 egg white, slightly beaten

Combine all ingredients, and freeze according to Basic Instructions.

\* To prepare cherry juice, remove stems and blossom ends from washed cherries. Cover 2 pounds of cherries with just enough water to cover. Simmer gently until cherries are soft—about 25 minutes. Strain the juice through a sieve lined with clean cheesecloth or a clean flour sack. If necessary, add water to make up 2 cups.

## PERSIMMON SHERBET

2 cups ripe persimmon pulp purée
1 cup orange juice
1/2 cup sugar
3 cups evaporated milk

Prepare puréed persimmons by forcing seeded fruit through a ricer or food mill, or by running in an electric blender. Add orange juice, sugar, and evaporated milk. Freeze according to Basic Instructions.

## PINEAPPLE SHERBET

1 cup sugar
2 cups water
2 cups crushed pineapple
2 cups light cream

Boil sugar and water together five minutes. Chill. Mix in pineapple and light cream. Freeze according to Basic Instructions.

## SHERBET RECIPES

### GREEN MANGO SHERBET

2 cups thick green mango sauce
1/3 cup lime juice
3 cups milk
1 egg white
2 cups sugar
3/4 cup hot water

To prepare green mango sauce, peel and slice about 3 pints of green mangoes, and cook with 1 cup of water until soft. Mash well, or force through a food mill. Chill.

Mix the mango sauce, lime juice, milk, slightly beaten egg white, and the sugar which has been dissolved in the hot water. Freeze according to Basic Instructions.

### RIPE MANGO SHERBET

1 tablespoon gelatin
1/4 cup cold water
1/2 cup boiling water
1/4 cup lime juice
3 cups ripe mango pulp, puréed
1 cup sugar

Sprinkle the gelatin over the 1/4 cup of cold water to soften. Stir in the hot water till gelatin is dissolved. Stir in the lime juice, and then mix well with the mango purée and the sugar. Freeze according to Basic Instructions.

## WATERMELON SHERBET

> 4 cups sieved watermelon pulp
> 2 6-oz. cans frozen lemonade concentrate
>   (pink, if possible)
> 2 lemonade cans of water (1$^1$/$_2$ cups)
> 4 egg whites, stiffly beaten

To sieve watermelon pulp, cut in chunks, remove all seeds, and press pulp through sieve or food mill. Or run chunks of pulp together with lemonade concentrate in an electric blender. Combine pulp, lemonade, and water. Begin freezing according to Basic Instructions. Add beaten egg whites after about five minutes, and continue freezing.

## TAMARIND SHERBET

> 2 cups water
> 1 cup sugar
> 2 cups tamarind pulp*
> 1 tablespoon lemon juice
> 2 egg whites
> 1/8 teaspoon salt

Combine water and sugar, and bring to a boil. Boil for five minutes. Chill. Add tamarind pulp and lemon juice. Freeze according to Basic Instructions until mixture is half frozen, or mushy. Beat egg whites and salt stiff. Fold into tamarind mixture. Finish freezing.

* Remove shells from tamarinds. Soak in water for several hours. Remove seeds.

## TOPPING RECIPES

### MINT SHERBET

2 cups sugar
2 cups water
1 cup chopped fresh mint leaves
1/4 cup lemon juice
1 cup orange juice
1/8 teaspoon salt
1/4 cup corn syrup
Few drops green coloring (optional)

Bring sugar and water to a boil. Remove from heat, and allow to cool to lukewarm. Mix in the mint leaves and lemon juice. Mash the mint leaves around in the syrup with a wooden spoon. Let mixture stand for an hour or so. Strain out the mint leaves. Add the orange juice, salt, and corn syrup to the mint-flavored syrup. Add green coloring, if desired. Chill. Freeze according to Basic Instructions.

# Toppings

SHOULD YOU WANT to gild the lily and dress up your ice cream with a topping, there's no need to sprint to the store for jars of commercial sundae sauce. Look around your own kitchen to see what you have on hand.

## SPRINKLES

All kinds of unexpected things can be sprinkled lightly on ice cream. Children are frequently partial to various crumbled cereals, especially the sugared kind, on their ice cream. Grape nuts and corn flakes are old favorites, as are chopped, toasted nuts of all kinds, from peanuts to pecans, from almonds to macadamias. Chopped up semi-sweet or sweet chocolate does delightful things to orange as well as to vanilla ice cream. Minced candied fruit makes a colorful touch. And don't forget crumbled macaroons, or toasted coconut.

## SAUCES

When you're in a hurry, there are some easy ones on the pantry shelf. How about the bottle of maple syrup —wouldn't that be a lovely touch on vanilla or nut ice cream? Honey lends itself well to the flavors of many fruit ice creams. The syrup drained from many canned fruits can be emphasized with a bit of lemon juice and thickened with a little cornstarch and used as ice cream sauce. Liqueurs and cordials, spooned over ice cream "as is," turn ordinary meals into fiestas.

## CHOCOLATE SAUCE

6 squares bitter chocolate, broken in pieces
2 cups sugar
1/2 cup butter
1 large can evaporated milk
1/8 teaspoon salt
1 teaspoon vanilla

**45**

## TOPPING RECIPES

Combine chocolate, sugar, butter, milk, and salt. Cook, stirring, over low burner until chocolate is melted and all ingredients are blended. Add vanilla. Serve hot or cold.

### BUTTERSCOTCH SAUCE

$1^1/_2$ cups brown sugar
1/2 cup dark corn syrup
4 tablespoons butter
3/4 cup heavy cream or evaporated milk

Combine brown sugar, corn syrup, and butter in heavy saucepan. Bring to a boil and boil gently to soft ball stage. (A drop in cold water will form a soft ball.) Stir in cream. Serve warm.

### CARAMEL CREAM SAUCE

1/2 pound caramels
1 cup evaporated milk

Place caramels and evaporated milk in the top of a double boiler, over gently boiling water. Stir occasionally until caramels melt and sauce is blended. Serve warm.

### CHOCOLATE SATIN SAUCE

1 package chocolate instant pudding
1 cup light corn syrup
3 tablespoons cream or evaporated milk

Stir pudding mix into corn syrup. Blend in cream.

### BUTTERSCOTCH SATIN SAUCE

> 1 package butterscotch instant pudding
> 3/4 cup chilled evaporated milk or light cream
> 3/4 cup light corn syrup

Mix pudding into evaporated milk with a fork, until just blended. Blend in the corn syrup.

### JAM SAUCE

> 1/2 cup apricot, strawberry, or raspberry jam
> 1/4 cup sugar
> 1 cup water
> 1 tablespoon brandy

Blend jam, sugar, and water and boil gently for two minutes. Stir in brandy. Serve warm or cold.

### FRUIT SAUCES

Most of us know that fresh ripe fruits and berries, peeled, sliced, and sugared, make delightful toppings for ice creams. Canned fruits can serve the same purpose. And don't forget the baby food shelf! A jar of apricot purée or chopped peaches makes a perfect ice cream sauce—especially if the flavor is perked up with a spoonful of brandy.

## TOPPING RECIPES

### ORANGE SAUCE

1/2 cup orange marmalade
1/2 cup orange juice

Blend in small pan. Bring to a boil and boil gently for about 2 minutes. Serve warm or chilled.

### CHERRY SAUCE

1 tablespoon cornstarch
1/4 cup sugar
1 large can pitted Bing cherries
1/4 cup Burgundy

Mix sugar and cornstarch well in a small pan. Drain in the cherry juice and blend. Bring to a boil over low heat, stirring constantly, and boil for two minutes. Mix well and serve warm.

### TANGERINE BRANDY SAUCE

1 cup tangerine juice
1/2 cup sugar
2 cups tangerine sections
1/4 cup brandy

Bring tangerine juice and sugar to a boil, and simmer for about five minutes. Gently mix in tangerine sections and brandy. Serve hot over ice cream.

# INDEX

# INDEX

## INDEX

## INDEX

## INDEX